Facilitator's Guide

Third Edition

Stirring the Head, Heart, AND Soul

Redefining Curriculum, Instruction, and Concept-Based Learning

H. LYNN ERICKSON

CORWIN PRESS
A SAGE Company

For information:

Corwin Press
A SAGE Company
2455 Teller Road
Thousand Oaks, California 91320
www.corwinpress.com

SAGE India Pvt. Ltd.
B 1/I 1 Mohan Cooperative Industrial Area
Mathura Road, New Delhi 110 044
India

SAGE Ltd.
1 Oliver's Yard
55 City Road
London EC1Y 1SP
United Kingdom

SAGE Asia-Pacific Pte. Ltd.
33 Pekin Street #02-01
Far East Square
Singapore 048763

Printed in the United States of America

ISBN 978-1-4129-6627-6

This book is printed on acid-free paper.

08 09 10 11 12 10 9 8 7 6 5 4 3 2 1

Acquisitions Editor:	Cathy Hernandez
Editorial Assistant:	Ena Rosen and Sarah Bartlett
Production Editor:	Eric Garner
Copy Editor:	Codi Bowman
Typesetter:	C&M Digitals (P) Ltd.
Proofreader:	Charlotte Waisner
Cover Designer:	Karine Hovsepian

Contents

About the Author   v

Introduction   1
    How to Use the Guide   1
    Additional Resources for Facilitators   2

Workshop Overview   3
    Guiding Questions   3
    Facilitator Introduction   4

Chapter-by-Chapter Study Guide: Facilitator's Guide to
    Stirring the Head, Heart, and Soul: Redefining Curriculum,
    Instruction, and Concept-Based Learning, **Third Edition,**
    by H. Lynn Erickson   5

    1. Making Change in a Changing World   5
        Summary   5
        Discussion Questions   6
        Learning Experiences   7
        Journal Writing Prompts   7
        Practical Applications   7
        Extending Facilitator Learning   7

    2. Concept-Based Curriculum   8
        Summary   8
        Discussion Questions   8
        Learning Experiences   8
        Journal Writing Prompts   11
        Practical Applications   11
        Extending Facilitator Learning   11

    3. State Academic Standards and Local Curriculum
        Frameworks   11
        Summary   11
        Discussion Questions   13
        Learning Experiences   13
        Journal Writing Prompts   14
        Practical Applications   14
        Extending Facilitator Learning   14

4. Designing Interdisciplinary, Integrated Curricula   **14**
Summary   14
Discussion Questions   15
Learning Experiences   15
Journal Writing Prompts   18
Practical Applications   18
Extending Facilitator Learning   19

5. Concept-Based Units: Samples and Questions   **19**
Summary   19
Discussion Questions   19
Learning Experiences   20
Journal Writing Prompts   24
Practical Applications   24
Extending Facilitator Learning   25

6. Assessing and Reporting Student Progress   **25**
Summary   25
Discussion Questions   26
Learning Experiences   26
Journal Writing Prompts   28
Practical Applications   28
Extending Facilitator Learning   28

7. Concept-Based Instruction   **28**
Summary   28
Discussion Questions   29
Learning Experiences   29
Journal Writing Prompts   31
Practical Applications   31
Extending Facilitator Learning   32

**8. Stirring the Head, Heart, and Soul:
Creating a Love of Learning**   **32**
Summary   32
Discussion Questions   32
Learning Experiences   33
Journal Writing Prompts   34
Practical Applications   34
Extending Facilitator Learning   35

Resources   **36**

Sample Workshop Agendas   **66**

Workshop Evaluation Form   **71**

About the Author

H. Lynn Erickson is an independent consultant assisting schools and districts with concept-based curriculum and instruction. Lynn is also the author of *Concept-Based Curriculum and Instruction for the Thinking Classroom* © 2007, Corwin Press. Lynn and Ken Erickson live in Washington State. They have two children and two grandchildren who stir her heart and soul.

Introduction

This guide is designed to accompany the study of the book *Stirring the Head, Heart, and Soul: Redefining Curriculum, Instruction, and Concept-Based Learning*, Third Edition by H. Lynn Erickson. It offers a framework for guiding group facilitators involved in professional development workshops. It summarizes the main ideas of each chapter in the book and aids facilitators in leading the change to a concept-based model for curriculum and instruction. The guide suggests discussion questions, workshop learning experiences, and journal writing prompts to process the information. Resources, which may be used as both handouts and overheads, provide the workshop facilitator with additional support material.

For **independent study**, participants may wish to follow these steps:

1. Read each chapter in the book.
2. Reflect on (or answer) the discussion questions.
3. Complete suggested learning experiences using related resources.

For **small study groups**, facilitators can guide the participants to follow these steps:

1. Read the assigned chapter in the book in advance.
2. Reflect on (or answer) the discussion questions.
3. Reflect on the resources during discussions.
4. Take part in the learning experiences using the resources.

For **small- or large-group workshops**, facilitators may wish to follow these steps:

1. Assign a different chapter to be read by each member in study groups of eight people to be shared at the beginning of Day 2 in a two-day workshop; or . . .

2. Request that all participants read Chapters 2 and 4 in advance of the workshop to gain some prior background.
3. Develop a short presentation on the main ideas of each chapter to use in conjunction with the suggested learning experiences.
4. Engage participants in answering the discussion questions.
5. Involve group members in one or more of the learning experiences for each chapter.

Additional Resources for Facilitators

Corwin Press also offers a free 16-page resource titled *Tips for Facilitators* that includes practical strategies and tips for guiding a successful meeting. The information in this section describes different professional development opportunities, the principles of effective professional development, some characteristics of an effective facilitator, the responsibilities of the facilitator, and practical tips and strategies to make the meeting more successful. *Tips for Facilitators* is available for free download at the Corwin Press Web site (www.corwinpress.com, under "Resources").

We recommend that facilitators download a copy of *Tips for Facilitators* and review the characteristics and responsibilities of facilitators and the professional development strategies for different types of work groups and settings.

Workshop Overview

✓ What are the goals you hold for your students?
✓ How is knowledge structured, and how can we use that structure to improve teaching and learning for all students and help you more effectively meet your goals?
✓ What is the difference between a *topic* and a *concept?*
✓ How do we write a generalization (enduring, essential understanding)?
✓ What is the difference between a *fact* and a *generalization?*
✓ How can we use a "conceptual lens" to engage higher levels of thinking, motivate students for learning, and differentiate for different ability levels?
✓ How can we incorporate concept-based strategies in the design of instructional units?

Additional Guiding Questions for One- and Two-Day Workshops

✓ What is "synergistic thinking," and how can teachers effect this kind of thinking?
✓ How do we scaffold thinking to write more powerful, enduring, essential understandings (generalizations) to teach toward?
✓ How can we use scaffolding to develop the thinking abilities of our students?
✓ How do we write different kinds of questions (factual, conceptual, and provocative) to guide students in their thinking?

Additional Guiding Questions for a Two-Day Workshop

✓ What does concept-based instruction "look like?"
✓ How can we adapt traditional graphic organizers to make them concept based?

✓ How can we adapt learning experiences for students to make them concept based?

✓ How do we design a concept-based unit of instruction?

Facilitator Introduction

✓ Open the workshop by thanking everyone for attending in order to learn new ways to help children learn. Review the workshop overview of guiding questions which are posted.

✓ Then ask participants to do a five-minute "free write" on the first question—the goals for their students. Ask for volunteers to share out loud and listen for three goals to reinforce: meeting standards for content and skills, demonstrating ability to think well, and becoming a motivated, lifelong learner.

✓ Tell participants that they will be learning how knowledge is structured and how we can use that structure to significantly improve teaching and learning. Tell them that they will also be learning specific instructional strategies that they can immediately apply in their classrooms to develop the thinking abilities of their students and to increase their motivation for learning.

Chapter-by-Chapter Study Guide

Facilitator's Guide to *Stirring the Head, Heart, and Soul: Redefining Curriculum, Instruction, and Concept-Based Learning,* Third Edition

by H. Lynn Erickson

Chapter 1. Making Change in a Changing World

Summary

Under pressure from the government, business, parents, and the media, schools struggle valiantly to improve education for students. But the improvement of education requires a high degree of cooperation and communication between the schools, government, business, and parents, and these entities can have different and, at times, conflicting perspectives on how to improve schools.

School districts that employ systems thinking (Senge, 1999, 2006) understand the complexity involved in bringing all the component parts of a learning organization together to raise achievement levels and improve education for all students. Professional learning communities (Dufour, Eaker, & DuFour, 2005) provide a logical starting place for school change because they offer a collaborative model for identifying and solving problems and planning for positive change.

In this book, Erickson makes the case for five additional changes that she feels are critical for improving education:

1. Develop a national concept-based curriculum model developed under knowledgeable guidance by teacher teams of the best disciplinary experts representing each grade level and subject area. This model of classroom-based units would be offered to school districts for voluntary use and could be adapted as needed to fit local needs.

2. Move away from curriculum frameworks driven by verb-driven objectives to clear statements of what students must *understand* (conceptually), *know* (factually by key topics), and be *able to do* in skills and processes.

3. Elevate teachers and administrators to professional status by raising pay scales to obtain high-quality applicants.

4. Provide far more time for inservice staff development. Teachers and administrators need at least two weeks each summer or one day per month to develop greater expertise in their discipline, in instructional pedagogy, in classroom management, and/or in child development.

5. Provide common planning time for teachers in a grade level or subject area. When teachers work together to plan for instruction they feel greater ownership in the curriculum and experience greater joy in teaching.

Discussion Questions

1. How well does your school district meet the idea of a "shared vision" described by Peter Senge (2006) on page 17 of the book? In what ways could a shared vision be strengthened for your school district?

2. If your school's "professional learning community" (DuFour et al., 2005) was going to meet on the topic of raising student achievement, what agenda items do you imagine would be contributed by the group?

3. As a teacher, why would you find it more helpful to be given a document that states what students must *know* factually, *understand* conceptually, and be *able to do* in skills and processes rather than receiving a traditional framework of verb-driven curriculum objectives?

4. What case can be made for elevating the professional status of teachers and administrators in relation to improved education for students?

5. Educators in countries that outscore the United States in academic tests spend far more time in mentorships and inservice training. What case can you make for increasing the staff development and mentorship opportunities in your school district?
6. How many areas of need can you suggest for staff development training?

Learning Experiences

Debating Ideas

Note to facilitator: This learning experience could replace or be done in conjunction with the discussion questions.

Time: 20 minutes
Materials: Chart paper and a marking pen

Ask participants to form groups of three to five people, and select one of the following topics based on the reading of Chapter 1. Debate the pros and cons, and be ready to summarize your thoughts for the entire audience of participants:

- A national (or state) concept-based curriculum of classroom units aligned to the major topics, concepts, and processes/ skills outlined in national standards (for voluntary use by school districts)
- Professional learning communities at each school in a district
- An increase in staff development time for educators to two full weeks per summer or one day per month

Journal Writing Prompts

If you were appointed the secretary of education for your school district, what steps would you take to improve education for all tudents?

Practical Applications

Develop a passionate proposal to start a professional learning community at your school. Provide supporting details for your key points. Present the proposal to your principal or staff.

Extending Facilitator Learning

DuFour, R., Eaker, R., & DuFour, R. (Eds.). (2005). *On common ground: The power of professional learning communities.* Bloomington, IN: The Solution Tree.
Senge, P. M. (1999). *The dance of change: The challenge of sustaining momentum in learning organizations.* New York: Doubleday.
Senge, P. M. (2006). *The fifth discipline: The art and practice of the learning organization.* New York: Doubleday.

Chapter 2. Concept-Based Curriculum

Summary

Chapter 2 contrasts the traditional topic-based curriculum with the more intellectually powerful concept-based curriculum. Erickson discusses the early concept-based work of Hilda Taba (1966) and extends the understanding of concepts and generalizations by framing them with the structure of knowledge. Definitions and examples of concepts and generalizations clarify the importance of defining and understanding the conceptual structure for curricula.

Discussion Questions

1. Why is it important for all teachers to understand how knowledge is structured?
2. How can this understanding elevate the quality of instruction?
3. Why does preK–Grade 12 curriculum need a conceptual structure in addition to a topic/skill structure?
4. How does a concept-based model develop deeper levels of understanding?
5. How does a concept-based model develop higher levels of thinking?

Learning Experiences

● *The Structure of Knowledge*

Time: 20 minutes
Materials: Resource 1—Structure of Knowledge, Resource 2—Structure of Knowledge Examples, and Resource 3—Blank Structure of Knowledge

Refer participants to the Structure of Knowledge, Figure 2.2 on page 31 in the book. Show Resource 1. Tell participants that knowledge has a structure just as the plant and animal kingdoms have structures. Using the background information on pages 30–41 in the book as well as the definitions of *concept* and *universal generalization* found in the Glossary on pages 249–250, explain the structure of knowledge components.

1. Tell participants that there is a theory level, and we teach theories in class, but we have so much work to do with the concepts and generalization levels that we can leave the theories on the back burner for now. (If asked, a theory is an idea supported by our best evidence to date, but it remains yet to be completely proven.)

2. Explain to participants that generalizations and principles are both statements of conceptual relationship, but they have a slight difference. Principles are the cornerstone, foundational "truths" of a discipline. They never have a qualifier (*often, can,* or *may*) in the sentence. A generalization may have a qualifier if the idea is important, but it does not hold in all cases. The laws of science and the axioms of mathematics are "principles." There are far more generalizations than principles in any discipline. Tell participants that they need not worry about differentiating generalizations from principles in their unit development, as both are statements of conceptual relationship and may simply be referred to as "generalizations," "enduring understandings," or "essential understandings."

Review Resource 2—Structure of Knowledge Examples with participants. Tell them that the "topic" is locked in time, place, or situation. (The exception is mathematics, which is a concept-based language. Therefore, mathematics topics are really broader concepts that are broken into subconcepts.

Ask participants to use Resource 3 to think of four concepts that they could teach through a topic they name on Line 1. Tell them concepts must fit the criteria on pages 34–35 (Concept Definition Test). Then ask participants to use just two of the concepts from Line 2 to complete the generalization statement on Line 3 of the resource. (Generalizations can contain more than two concepts, but for this learning experience the task is simplified by designating two concepts.) Tell participants to retain the word *that* in the stem starter to avoid writing a traditional content "objective." Remind participants that Line 3 needs to be an idea supported by the facts that can transfer through time, across cultures, and across situations.

Have participants share out loud Line 1 and Line 3. Give suggestions if needed.

Ask these questions:

Where should we ultimately target our teaching in a concept-based classroom?

(Answer: to the level of the concepts and generalizations)

What is the role of the fact base in a concept-based lesson?

(Answer: to support the deeper conceptual understandings—generalizations)

What is the major difference between the topics/facts and concepts/generalizations?

(Answer: Concepts and generalizations transfer; topics and facts are locked in time, place, or situation.)

Note to facilitator: A common error in writing generalizations is the use of passive voice ("is affected by," etc.). If you hear this error when participants share their Line 3 generalization, suggest they "flip" their sentence by putting the end of the sentence at the beginning. This will make the verb active—*affects.*

Concept or Topic?

Time: 15 minutes
Materials: Resource 4—Topic or Concept

Ask participants to follow these directions:

- Refer to Resource 4 and underline all the topics in the list of concepts and topics. Use the criteria for a concept (pp. 34 and 36) to base your decisions. Tell them to share which are topics in their work groups.
- Tell participants to look at the bottom of the resource and independently write three other *topics* for their grade level or subject area and three other *concepts.*
- Refer participants back to the list of topics/concepts and ask them to circle two macroconcepts that transfer widely across subject areas—and underline two microconcepts that reflect the content of a particular discipline.

Universal Generalizations

Time: 15 minutes
Materials: Resource 5—Supporting Universal Generalizations

For each of the three universal generalizations on Resource 5, have participants brainstorm as many factual examples as they can think of. Tell them they have 15 minutes to complete the work. Ask groups to share out loud without repeating examples that have already been given. Discuss the value of "idea-centered" instruction with the total audience.

Note to facilitator: Teaching to universal generalizations is idea-centered because generalizations require factual support to be understood. Teaching to ideas requires a higher level of synergistic (factual/conceptual thinking).

Visual Interpretations

Time: 30 minutes
Materials: Resource 6—Visual Interpretations, chart paper (one piece per work group), and colored marking pens of various colors at each table.

Have participants collaborate in their work group of three to five people, and create a visual interpretation of each statement on Resource 6. Ask them to partner with another table and share visual interpretations by explaining pictures in relation to the statements.

Journal Writing Prompts

Using your own language, describe the difference between a traditional topic-based curriculum/instruction model and the higher level, concept-based model.

Reflect on your own teaching in relationship to concept-based instruction. Where would you place yourself on a scale of 1 to 10 with 10 being a confident concept-based teacher? What are your next steps in moving forward on the concept-based teaching continuum?

Practical Applications

Take a set of your state's academic standards for your grade level. Underline all of the concepts in one color and all of the topics in another color. If you teach history and find that most of your standards are topics, make a list of related concepts for some of your important topics.

Extending Facilitator Learning

Erickson, H. (2007). *Concept-based curriculum and instruction for the thinking classroom.* Thousand Oaks, CA: Sage.

Taba, H. (1966). *Teaching strategies and cognitive functioning in elementary schoolchildren. Cooperative research project.* Washington, DC: Office of Education, U.S. Department of Health, Education, and Welfare.

Wiggins, G., & McTighe, J. (2005). *Understanding by design* (expanded 2nd ed.). Alexandria, VA: Association for Supervision and Curriculum Development.

Chapter 3. State Academic Standards and Local Curriculum Frameworks

Summary

State academic standards frame the curricula in local school districts. The focus on standards has increased attention on curriculum, instruction, and student achievement. This focus benefits education. But to make the greatest gains for students, local school districts need to understand how to address shortfalls in the design of state academic standards.

State standards vary in the degree of specificity. Some standards are detailed objectives that reflect specific content; others are broad, general objectives that can be met through a wide variety of content. Another difference in standards can be seen in the design of the various disciplines. History standards are more often topic based and fact driven; science standards are concept based and conceptually driven; and mathematics standards are skill driven. This means that school districts need to bring design coherence across the different disciplines at the local level.

Design coherence means that each discipline adheres to a tripartite model of conceptual understanding, factual knowledge, and processes/skills. Therefore, curricula at the local level needs to draw out (and sometimes infer) from the state standards what students must understand, know, and be able to do. This means that when working with history standards, committee members will need to identify the important concepts and generalizations (the transferable lessons of history) related to the required topics. When working with science standards, committee members will need to identify factual examples and specific applications to support the concepts, principles, and generalizations delineated in the state standards. And when working with mathematics, committee members will need to identify the concepts and subconcepts embedded within the skills of state standards—and put the concepts into statements of conceptual relationship to provide supportive understandings for the skills.

Scope and sequence charts are helpful in delineating skill development through the grade levels. For mathematics, the skill sequence should be accompanied by a set of related conceptual understandings (generalizations) since mathematics is a conceptual language. We don't just "do" mathematics; we need to "understand" the conceptual relationships of mathematics.

This chapter suggests that curriculum mapping is a valuable first step in beginning curriculum work at the local level. Curriculum maps ask teachers to identify the topics and skills they are currently teaching for each calendar month. The curriculum maps can then be refined and aligned with the state academic standards and expectations. Curriculum maps allow schools to identify content that needs to be discarded or added, and they highlight gaps and redundancies in content.

When teachers feel that they have too much content for a course or subject area, they can create a "concept/content matrix." The matrix correlates specific topics in a curriculum to macro- and microconcepts. To reduce the overloaded curriculum, teachers can focus on fewer examples to illustrate a particular concept, or they can reduce the number of specific concepts being addressed in the course.

Discussion Questions

Use "Extending Thought" questions on page 67 in book

Learning Experiences

● *Examining the Design of State Academic Standards*

Time: 30 minutes

Materials: Sample set of state academic standards for mathematics, science, social studies, and English/language arts (could be just a page from one grade level for each subject area or subject specific for a focused workshop) *Note:* Download local state standard samples from the Internet.

Ask work groups of three to five people to compare the design across the four subject areas. Which one is concept based? Topic based? Skill based? Direct the participants to take the mathematics, science, and social studies standards and work together to identify a conceptual structure for each subject area example by following one or more of these steps:

1. Begin with science since this is likely concept based. Identify a conceptual understanding (a generalization: a statement of relationship between two or more concepts). Example: Organisms adapt to changing environments.

2. Choose a performance indicator from the history standards that names a specific topic. Ask why students should study the topic and finish the phrase, ("in order to understand that . . ." with a transferable generalization (understanding).
   Example: Analyze European exploration to the New World during the 1800s in order to understand that . . . *nations explore new lands to gain wealth, power, and prestige.*

3. Choose a performance indicator from the mathematics standards. Ask why students should perform the skill and write the deeper conceptual understanding following the skill by again completing the phrase "in order to understand that . . ."
   Example: Use angle measurements to classify angles as acute, obtuse, or right—in order to understand that . . . *the arc of an angle, measured in degrees, indicates whether the angle is acute, obtuse, or right.*

Ask work groups to discuss the value of bringing conceptual coherence to curriculum designs across subject areas.

Journal Writing Prompts

You are in charge of leading a committee to develop a *tripartite* curriculum for a particular subject area in your school district. Develop a set of steps to share with your committee explaining how they will work with your state's academic standards to create the tripartite curriculum.

Practical Applications

Choose one or more of the following tasks to develop curriculum in your school district or classroom:

1. Complete a curriculum map for one or more subject areas. Align the map to state academic standards.
2. Develop a tripartite curriculum for at least one grade level or course that identifies what students must understand (conceptually), know (factually), and be able to do in processes and skills.

Extending Facilitator Learning

Hayes-Jacobs, H. (Ed.). (2004). *Getting results with curriculum mapping*. Alexandria, VA: Association for Supervision and Curriculum Development.

Chapter 4. Designing Interdisciplinary, Integrated Curricula

Summary

Is integration what we do with subjects, or is it a cognitive process? In this chapter, the author proposes that *integration* is a cognitive process evidenced by the ability to see patterns and connections between the factual and conceptual levels of knowledge. Erickson clarifies the difference between *inter*disciplinary and *intra*disciplinary curricula and posits that both kinds of curriculum design can be "integrated" if there is a conceptual level of work involved that pulls the thinking beyond the facts.

Steps for designing a concept-based, integrated unit of study accompany a helpful template for laying out the unit components and related lesson plan. (Resource A in the book provides alternate unit templates.) The Chapter 4 section on questions and answers related to each of the unit design components provides specific help for the most commonly asked questions from teachers.

Discussion Questions

1. What is the difference between a "coordinated, multidisciplinary," and an "integrated, interdisciplinary" unit of study?
2. What is the critical element to create an integrated, interdisciplinary unit of three study? (Answer: the conceptual lens)
3. What are the benefits of *inter*disciplinary unit design?
4. What are the benefits of *intra*disciplinary unit design?
5. What are the dangers of forcing different subject areas at the secondary level into interdisciplinary work *for the majority* of their units?
6. Why are quality teacher-designed units of instruction preferable to solely textbook-driven instruction?
7. How can the process of "scaffolding generalizations" be used with students to deepen and clarify their understanding of content?
8. Why do guiding questions need to be a mix of factual, conceptual, and provocative (debatable)? What is the problem if questions are only debatable?
9. How does a performance task (of deep understanding) draw on an important generalization in its design? (Answer: the performance [the "how"] needs to include the language of the generalization to bridge the performance to the conceptual level of deeper understanding.)

Learning Experiences

● *Designing a Unit of Study*

Materials: Resource 7—Unit Design Steps from page 75 of book (Refer participants to page 75 in book.), Resource 8—A blank copy of the Unit Design Template on pages 76–83 for laying out all of the unit components, explanations for each unit design step on pages 85–102 for facilitator reference, easel paper, and a marking pen for each table group for designing the unit web and generalizations.

This chapter provides a step-by-step guide for designing a concept-based unit of study.

The unit work begins with the design of a Unit Web (either interdisciplinary or intradisciplinary in design). The training on the structure of knowledge and its components are important prior learnings and can be explored during the first morning of a two-day workshop. The design of a unit can begin with the web during the afternoon of the first day. The presenter will likely be able to accomplish Steps 1, 2, and 4 on page 75 in the book during the first afternoon. (Leave Step 3, the Unit Overview until the end of the design process since time is limited.) The unit design steps correspond to the template on pages 76–82. The unit can be broken down into lesson plans using the template on pages 83–84. Day 2 would begin with refining Step 4, the Unit Generalizations, to ensure that they are clear and powerful. Then proceed to the Guiding Questions in Step 5 of the design process.

Note to facilitator: If you are holding a one-day workshop or will not be leading the design of a complete instructional unit, the following learning experiences are suggested to reinforce strategies that benefit classroom instruction as well as unit design:

● *Choosing a Conceptual Lens*

Time: 20 minutes
Materials: Resource 9—Sample Conceptual Lenses, tag strip, and a colored marker for each table

Show Resource 9, and tell participants that selecting a concept to use as a "conceptual lens" when studying a topic provides students with a focus for deeper thinking about the topic, engages their interest in the study, and allows them to transfer knowledge at the conceptual level.

Divide the total group in half. Direct half the room to write a specific topic that is locked in time, place, or situation on their tag strip with a colored marker. Topic examples could be the presidential election, the Iraq war, Picasso, global warming, the U.S. economy today, our pets, cloning . . .

Direct the other half of the room to number off and choose a conceptual lens from Resource 9 on their tag strip with a colored marker.

Have everyone stand. Topics are to find a suitable "conceptual lens" to be their partner within 20 seconds. Explain to your lens how you think they could enrich your message. Now it is the "lenses" turn. Look for another topic and switch partners. Tell your new topic how you could enrich whatever they have to say.

Ask the topics to be seated. Ask the lenses to stand side by side facing the topics. Ask the topics to select three suitable lenses for their topic that could provide students with a choice of lens.

● *Writing Generalizations*

Time: 20 minutes
Materials: Academic standards and sample pages from each core area subject

Chapter 5 in the book shows many examples of unit webs. These webs are the best way to identify concepts for writing generalizations, but this learning experience provides an alternative way to identify concepts if you do not wish to use the learning experience "Designing a Unit Web" from Chapter 5 at this point.

Provide participants with a sample page from academic standards related to content expectations (social studies, science, or mathematics). Ask participants to underline all concepts they find on the page. If the history standards list only topics, ask participants to draw out related concepts from some of the topics and write them in the margins.

Ask participants to complete the stem, "Students understand that . . ." putting two or more of the concepts from their standards into a sentence of relationship. The sentence must be a statement that transfers through time, across cultures, or across situations to be a generalization. The generalization needs to be an important, transferable understanding that reflects the intent of the academic standard. Remind participants that since generalizations must transfer through time and across examples, they cannot contain any proper nouns or past tense verbs.

● *Scaffolding Generalizations*

Time: 30 minutes
Materials: Resource 10—Scaffolding Thinking to Complex Levels

Ask participants to write one more generalization using the concepts in their sample page of standards, but require that they use a Level 1 verb: *impact, affect, influence, is, are, have.* These Level 1 verbs produce a weaker generalization.

Ask participants to scaffold to a stronger Level 2 statement by flipping the Level 1 generalization into a "how" or "why" question. Answering the question using more specific concepts will clarify the idea.

Suggest that participants can scaffold to a Level 3 idea for advanced students, or for all students if they wish, by asking, "So what . . . is the effect or significance (of the Level 2 idea)?" Share scaffolding by pairing tables or have each table share out loud if the total group is not too large. (Examples of scaffolding can be found on pages 89–90 of the book.)

Tell participants that we should drop Level 1 generalizations in our instruction because they are unclear and lack conceptual depth and specificity. Tell them we want to teach to the clarity and power of Level 2 generalizations, and we want to challenge some or all students at times to Level 3 generalizations. Rule of thumb: Two-thirds of the generalizations in a unit of instruction would be Level 2, and one-third would be Level 3. Another rule of thumb: Elementary grade level units need 5–8 generalizations per unit; secondary grade level units need 8–10 generalizations per unit.

● *Guiding Questions*

Time: 20 minutes
Materials: Resource 11—Guiding Questions

Review the description of the different kinds of guiding questions on Resource 11. Ask participants to write a mixed set of three to five factual and conceptual questions to guide students to one of the generalizations developed in the previous learning experience on writing generalizations. Call for people to read out loud their factual and conceptual questions. Then ask everyone to write a provocative (debate) question related to the overriding topic of the generalization.

● *Culminating Performance Task*

Time: 30 minutes
Materials: Resource 12—Writing a Performance Task

Review the completed example of a performance task found on pages 98 and 100 with the participants. Have participants create a performance task using Resource 12 (which is Figure 4.6 on page 99 in the book).

Ask work groups to switch tasks when they are completed and check to see that the group they are reviewing tied back to the "why" statement with their performance. Remind participants that the "language of the generalization" should appear in the performance to ensure the tie back.

Journal Writing Prompts

A concept-based unit of instruction differs from a traditional topic-based unit of instruction in the following ways:

_____

_____

_____

_____

Practical Applications

Design concept-based instructional units for your school district, your subject area, your grade level, or your classroom.

Employ the strategies learned in the design of units for classroom instruction to develop the thinking and understanding of your students.

Extending Facilitator Learning

Erickson, H. (2007). *Concept-based curriculum and instruction for the thinking classroom.* Thousand Oaks, CA: Sage.

Chapter 5. Concept-Based Units: Samples and Questions

Summary

Chapter 5 supports the unit design steps described in Chapter 4 by sharing examples of completed unit components for different grade levels and subject areas. Question and answer sections for elementary and secondary schools address common concerns in the design of interdisciplinary units of instruction. The chapter closes with a discussion of the International Baccalaureate Programme, which aligns with concept-based principles, and career and technical education programs, which this author fully supports.

Discussion Questions

1. Why is a "unit web" a useful tool when designing a concept-based unit?
   (Answer: to provide the critical concepts for writing unit generalizations [enduring, essential understandings])
2. Examine the social studies example on pages 136–137. What is the value of designing an elementary social studies curriculum in this manner? How is depth added to the traditional "expanding worlds" design with this model? What would be the effect if a second set of units retained the content but changed the lens to Interdependence? What if a final set of units changed the lens to Change and Continuity?
3. How can you "sell" the idea of designing an interdisciplinary unit of instruction in a middle school or high school?
4. What would be the danger at the secondary school level if interdisciplinary unit design were mandated for the majority of the year?
5. What kinds of school structures allow more flexibility in successfully creating interdisciplinary units at the secondary level?
6. How can elementary teachers ensure that interdisciplinary units maintain the integrity of each subject area brought into a study?
7. How can concepts aid in the program blending of academic with career and technical education? How does this blending enhance the education of students for the 21st century?

Learning Experiences

● *Designing a Unit Web*

Time: 30 minutes
Materials: Resource 13a—Elementary Grade Web, Resource 13b—Secondary Grade Level Web, Resource 14—Steps in Designing the Unit Web, paper, and a marking pen for each table group

Make certain participants are sitting in grade-level or subject-specific work groups of no more than five people to facilitate the design process.

Show an example of a concept-content web (page 120, Resource 13a for elementary teacher's workshop; page 131, Resource 13b for secondary teacher's workshop) and describe the component parts: unit title, conceptual lens, strands, subtopics, and subconcepts. Tell participants that a concept/content web is an excellent tool to use in identifying the concepts for writing enduring, essential understandings (generalizations) for a unit of study. It is the starting point in unit development. Tell participants that they will create a web for a unit they would like to teach. (Make certain that participants are seated by grade level or subject area for this learning experience.)

Show Resource 14, which lists the steps in designing the unit web:

1. Identify the *unit title* for the center circle on the web.
2. Identify a suitable *conceptual* lens to focus the unit work.
3. Identify the *strands* around the unit title.
4. List *subtopics* and *subconcepts* under each strand around the web.

Note to facilitator:

1. The conceptual lens and the subconcepts would be used to write unit generalizations. There will only be one or two generalizations using the lens to address *transferable breadth*; the other generalizations will be crafted with the subconcepts under each strand to provide *conceptual depth*.
2. The strands for a social studies web will always be history, geography, government, economics, and culture.
3. The strands for an interdisciplinary unit would represent different subject areas;
4. The strands for an intradisciplinary unit would be the major topics for the unit title.
5. Literature unit strands would be the title of books reflecting a genre unit title (e.g., historical fiction) and a particular conceptual lens (e.g., survival). If two or more books are used to reflect a genre or particular conceptual lens, each book would address the strands of *Literary Concepts*, *Reader's Craft*, and *Writer's Craft*.

Refer participants to page 35 for examples of the literature concepts for these strands. If the title of the unit was a particular book, the strands would be Literary Concepts, Reader's Craft, and Writer's Craft.

Point out the use of the conceptual lens to focus and deepen thinking about the topic. Tell participants that the conceptual lens is usually a broader (macro) concept such as Conflict, Interdependence, or System. The concepts under each strand around the web are called "subconcepts." The unit web should provide enough concepts to write 5–8 generalizations for an elementary unit and 8–10 generalizations for a secondary unit. The web should also show critical factual topics, although they would not be used to write generalizations.

For One-Day Workshops:
This part of the workshop offers the facilitator two options.

Learning Experiences

● *Option A—Instruction* and *Option B—Practice With Generalizations*

Time: 60 minutes for each option
Materials: Participants can work on 8½ × 11-inch notepaper and then transfer to the unit template (Resource 8) for the remaining unit components if the workshop extends to Day 2.

Option A—Instruction: Ask participants to pair up and decide who will read page 185 to the top of 200 and who will read pages 200–215. This chapter on concept-based instruction provides many classroom examples and adapted learning experiences. Tell participants that they will have a half hour to read their half of the chapter and then 15 minutes each to share what they learned with their partner. As facilitator, you are the timekeeper.

Option B—Practice with Generalizations: To further the practice with writing (and scaffolding) generalizations and guiding questions (Chapter 4 Learning Experiences), ask participants to use their concept/content web to write two or three generalizations using their conceptual lens (a unit can have one or two concepts as the lens, but no more), and then use the subconcepts under each strand to write their other generalizations. Tell participants that generalizations written with the macroconcepts (systems, order, change, etc.) provide *breadth* (greater transferability), and generalizations written with microconcepts (organism, scarcity, commutativity) provide *depth* (deeper conceptual understanding) to learning. Both macro and micro ideas are important.

Note to facilitator: For a two-day workshop, select Option B so that participants have additional practice with writing generalizations prior to the Day 2 work.

After the generalizations are completed direct participants to write a mix of three to five factual and conceptual questions for *each* generalization—(Chapter 4 Learning Experience Guiding Questions, Resource 11). Time may allow participants to work on only one of the question sets during Day 1 of the workshop, or question writing may need to be moved to Day 2. Remind participants that the purpose of the questions is to guide students from the facts to the related enduring understanding (generalization). Finally, ask participants to write one or two provocative (debate) questions for the entire unit.

Note to facilitator: For a two-day workshop, tell participants that you want them to form discussion groups of eight and you are going to release them 45 minutes early so they can each read a chapter from *Stirring the Head, Heart and Soul* (3rd ed.) for a presentation of key points in the morning. Allow about five minutes to form the groups of eight, and have each member choose a chapter. Tell them that the next morning they will each have 10 minutes to report on the key points from their chapter within their discussion group.

Note to facilitator: Save the unit webs and the generalizations from Day 1 to continue the unit design work on Day 2.

For two-day workshops—next steps
Tell participants that they will be completing their draft unit following the book study. Ask participants to gather in their book discussion groups.

Day 2 Learning Experiences

● *Book Discussion*

Time: 80 minutes
Materials: Book—*Stirring the Head, Heart and Soul* (3rd ed.)

Facilitator:
Welcome everyone back to Day 2 and tell them they will be sharing the chapter they read the previous evening, and then they will be working with their unit web group from Day 1 to draft the other components of a concept-based unit.

Begin the chapter sharing in the discussion groups. Let the audience know when each 10-minute time period ends so they can shift to the next chapter.

● *Unit Design Continued . . .*

Time: 4 hours

Materials: Unit web, generalizations, and guiding questions drafted on Day 1

Ask participants to return to their original unit design group (the web group) to continue the unit development. As the facilitator, it is your responsibility to interject instruction throughout the day and guide participants through each of the steps listed on page 75 in Chapter 4. Refer participants to the completed unit in the book, Resource D pages 243–248, if they need a model for different unit components. There are also examples of various components throughout the book.

Note to facilitator: You will pick up on Day 2 by having participants refine and add to the generalization and guiding questions. Pace the unit writing so that participants have had a chance to practice each of the steps by the end of the day.

1. Tell participants that the unit page asking for Critical Content (what students must KNOW) is the listing of key factual topics or summary statements of factual knowledge.
2. Tell participants that the Skills page is asking for the discrete and transferable skills required by the state standards for the subject and grade level. Tell participants they can pull these transferable skills directly from the standards. Caution them not to attach the transferable skills to a particular topic at this time but to wait until they develop the assessments and learning experiences for the unit.
3. Direct the participants to Resource 8 for laying out the unit design steps on a template.
4. Tell them that Resource A in the book contains different formats for a unit template.
5. When you get to the step of designing a (Culminating) Performance task, engage participants in the Chapter 4 Learning Experience—Culminating Performance Task using Resource 12. If you ask for volunteers to share with the group, ask the audience to identify how the performance ties back to the enduring, essential understanding. (Make certain the performance picks up the language from the generalization in the directions to students.)
6. If you have time, you may want participants to design a Scoring Guide for their performance task (see Learning Experience "The Scoring Guide" from Chapter 6).
7. If you do not have time, you need to direct them to the pages in the book that describe how to develop a scoring guide (pages 176–177). Tell them there are other models that are acceptable for scoring guides, but it is important to include the conceptual understanding as one of the criteria being assessed.

8. You may decide to simply describe the scoring guide and use remaining time to explain and practice the Wiggins and McTighe (2005) idea of "designing backward." Once the culminating performance task is written, explain that the Unit Learning Experiences for students are developed to prepare the students for success on the task and other assessments. Ask participants to write one or two learning experiences that would prepare the students for success on the culminating task. What knowledge and skills do students need before they are assessed on the task? Tell participants that even though the unit learning experiences are designed after the culminating performance task, they are taught prior to the task.

● *Workshop Close*

Time: 40 minutes
Materials: None

The unit design will take most of the day, but there will be time the last hour to discuss ways to support teachers in making the transition to concept-based instruction. As the facilitator you have the option of

1. using the last hour for a "walkabout" to share unit work from each group;
2. leading a discussion of interest to the group related to concept-based curriculum and instruction; or
3. engaging participants with the Chapter 8 Learning Experience, "Stirring the Creative Spirit."

Close the workshop with a summary of what was learned. Call for any remaining questions. Encourage participants to practice the strategies learned with their students and teach other colleagues what they learned in the workshop. Ask participants to complete the workshop evaluation.

Journal Writing Prompts

Ask participants to do a five-minute free write on everything they understand about the importance of concepts and generalizations at this point. Ask for some sharing with the total group. Call for any questions that may still be unclear to participants.

Practical Applications

Design a unit web on your own that pulls in the critical subtopics and subconcepts from your academic standards. When you feel comfortable with the alignment, use the subconcepts from your web to write five to eight unit generalizations to focus your teaching. Write only one or two generalizations using your conceptual lens. Write the other generalizations using subconcepts from around the web. DO NOT use the conceptual lens in every generalization as this becomes redundant and trite sounding.

Extending Facilitator Learning

Erickson, H. (2007). *Concept-based curriculum and instruction for the thinking classroom.* Thousand Oaks, CA: Sage.

Chapter 6. Assessing and Reporting Student Progress

Summary

Chapter 6 provides a brief comparison of normative- and criterion-referenced tests and then describes a variety of alternative assessments. Standards-based assessments, which measure benchmark progress, are a major focus in schools today. Authentic performance assessments that show what students can do with what they know are also are major design focus at the state, school district, and classroom levels today.

This chapter emphasizes the point that concept-based assessment is concerned with measuring deeper conceptual understanding in addition to factual knowledge. Therefore, assessment measures what students *know* (factually), *understand* (conceptually), and are *able to do* in skills and processes. Measuring just *know* and *able to do* is no longer sufficient.

This chapter supports the idea that areas such as reading and writing, which are marked by developmental indicators, need to be assessed according to progress along a continuum. Assessing and reporting process development is very different from assessing and reporting mastery of inert content. The indicators for process development need to show a *growth* continuum over time rather than a bell-shaped curve of deficits and strengths.

Since concept-based curriculum and instruction is vitally concerned with the development of thinking abilities, Chapter 6 includes information on assessing critical thinking and reasoning. Thinking and reasoning are developmental process skills that are too often neglected in instruction and assessment. The ability to think well needs to be developed just as reading and writing processes need to be developed. Assessment needs to engage students in metacognitive self-assessment of their work as part of the process so they internalize the criteria for quality work.

Sample scoring guides and criteria and technical requirements for quality rubrics round out the discussion of assessment.

Discussion Questions

1. When are criterion-referenced tests preferable to normative-referenced assessments in education?
2. Assessing factual knowledge is common, but how could one measure for deeper conceptual understanding?
   (Answer: Assess to the level of the generalization, requiring the use of facts as support.)
3. How would you describe a quality process assessment in reading, writing, or thinking?
4. Why is it important for teachers to be able to determine a student's instructional level, strengths, and weaknesses in reading or writing? Do you feel teachers in elementary and middle school have the requisite training in this area? Should teachers also be able to determine and develop a student's ability to think critically and conceptually?
5. What are some of the differences between a weak, poorly designed scoring guide and a strong, well-designed scoring guide?

Learning Experiences

● *Let's Talk Testing*

Time: 30 minutes
Materials: Easel paper and marking pen for presenter

Testing has become an "elephant in the classroom" because of the amount of time required for standards-based assessments, criterion-referenced assessments, and alternative assessments such as performance tasks. Lead participants in a discussion of this problem. Then pose the question, "How can we determine a better balance between testing and teaching?" Discuss, "If we examine our instruction, routines, and learning activities throughout a day, can we find examples of poor use of time?" (Presenter—list examples for discussion.)

● *A Thinking Rubric*

Time: 30 minutes
Materials: Resource 15—Standard Level Performances for Critical Thinking

Review the nine criteria for critical thinking developed by Richard Paul on pages 169–170 in the book. Ask participants to work in groups of three to six to describe what the "standard" level of performance would look like for each of Paul's nine criteria for critical thinking. Suggest that the participants pull key words out of the questions under each criterion on page 170 to help describe the standard level of performance.

Example: Clarity—the student work provides specific examples to illustrate meaning. Main ideas are elaborated with supporting details.

● *The Scoring Guide*

Time: 30 minutes

Materials: Resources16a—Scoring Guide, 16b—Scoring Guide for Primary Grade Task, and 16c—Scoring Guide for Task if Letter Grades Are Required

Note to facilitator: These resources can be used as handouts or overheads.

Direct participants to design a scoring guide using the four elements described on pages 174 and 175. If they do not have a performance task available, have them first develop a performance task (see Chapter 4 Learning Experience—Culminating Performance Task). Remind participants that the lower levels of the scale need to state what students can do *at that level,* de-emphasizing what they cannot do. The definition of a scoring guide is "progress toward a standard," so a model that states only what students *cannot do* is not indicative of growth and progress. Participants can use the blank format provided in Resource 16a or design a simpler scoring guide format incorporating the four elements on pages 174 and 175.

Resource 16a is a more complex scoring guide design. Four criteria are each defined according to indicators of performance for Levels 4, 3, 2, and 1. Remember to state Levels 1 and 2 with "can do, but not yet" language as much as possible. The standard for each criterion to meet proficiency is a Level 3. The total standard level of proficiency requires a score of 12. A completed example can be found on page 178 in the book.

Resources 16b and 16c are options for creating a less complex scoring guide to assess a performance task. Handout 16b is best used in the early grade levels, when letter grades are not required. The standard box lists what proficient would look like. If all proficiency criteria are checked, the student receives a rating of three.

If the student exceeds the criteria and demonstrates excellent performance, they are given a rating of 4. Examples of ways to exceed the standard are provided, but students are given credit if they exceed the standard in any number of ways—as long as all of the criteria in the standard box have been met.

Resource 16c is used when letter grades are required. The standard level of performance is clearly defined according to content (knowledge and understanding) and process (skill) expectations. The performance expectations answer the question, "What does it *look like* when done to standard." The teacher assigns points or percentages to each criterion and may weight criteria differently as long as the total equals 100. A scoring key defines the requisite points or percentages for different letter grades. An *I* indicates that the students cannot be scored because they are not yet approaching the standard.

Journal Writing Prompts

You are the new director of assessment in the Trouble School District. The superintendent and school board have requested a brief report on your views for a quality assessment program for the district. List the kinds of assessment you envision and write a short rationale for each. Include a paragraph that describes your views on classroom assessment—kinds, benefits, amount of time required, and cautions.

You are a classroom teacher concerned with the amount of time taken from instruction to carry out standards-based testing. Write a letter to your principal expressing your concerns related to the trade-off between testing and time for learning.

You are a school principal. Write a memo to your staff expressing your beliefs on the uses and value of the different kinds of testing used in your school.

Practical Applications

Create a scoring guide to assess the reading, writing, or thinking abilities of your class on a particular assignment.

Create a scoring guide, with clear criteria, to assess student work on a performance task you use in your classroom.

Extending Facilitator Learning

Popham, W. (2008). *Transformative assessment.* Alexandria, VA: Association for Supervision and Curriculum Development.
Wiggins, G. (1998). *Educative assessment: Designing assessments to inform and improve student performance.* San Francisco: Jossey-Bass.
Wiggins, G., & McTighe, J. (2005). *Understanding by design* (expanded 2nd ed.). Alexandria, VA: Association for Supervision and Curriculum Development.

Chapter 7. Concept-Based Instruction

Summary

Fact-based instruction places the emphasis on learning the facts related to specific topics. Knowledge related to the facts is the end goal. Concept-based instruction places the emphasis on learning the concepts, principles, and transferable ideas that arise from the study of significant topics and facts. Deeper conceptual under-standing supported by specific facts is the end goal. This means that concept-based instruction differs in a number of significant ways from topic-based instruction.

In this chapter, Erickson explores these differences and shares classroom examples of concept-based learning experiences from different grade levels and subject areas. She provides guidance in adapting learning experiences and curriculum tools, such as graphic organizers, to evoke conceptual thinking.

There are many popular initiatives in education today that sup-port concept-based instruction. Essential and guiding questions and differentiation of curriculum—when combined with concept-based instruction—become powerful initiatives that help scaffold student potential. An initiative that Erickson asks us to consciously bring back to education is the use of cooperative learning. This research-supported initiative is gathering dust in too many secondary schools. Yet it is a powerful tool in fostering language development, develop-ing conceptual and critical thinking, and motivating students for learning. Cooperative group tasks value the intellect of each child in the learning process. Cooperative groups reduce the overuse of straight rows of students watching the teacher do all the work.

Discussion Questions

Discuss the Extending Thought questions on pages 214–215 in the book.

Learning Experiences

● *Fact-Based Instruction Versus Concept-Based Instruction*

Time: 10–15 minutes
Materials: None

Tell the table groups that they will be dialoguing on the best approach for social studies instruction. Say, "Half of your table group are historians who believe that students must learn as many facts as possible to know history. The other half of your table are historians who believe students need to know the facts that sup-port the transferable lessons of history. For the next 10 to 15 min-utes, dialogue and support your position at the table on the best approach to teaching social studies." After the dialogue, share your reflections with the whole audience. Can you identify beliefs about social studies instruction that both groups of historians would support?

● *The Power of Cooperative Learning*

Time: 20 minutes
Materials: One blank sheet of copy paper per person plus one extra per table

Ask individual participants to take eight minutes and create a political cartoon about the 2008 presidential election. If artistically challenged, just write down the idea. Then ask participants to *work together* at their table to create another political cartoon on the blank piece of copy paper in the center of the table. Ask participants to reflect on the process when working together versus working independently. Make the points that cooperative learning generates better ideas, fosters the use of language, and is generally more motivating.

● *Asking Powerful Questions*

Time: 20 minutes
Materials: Easel paper and a marking pen per table group

Imagine that you have just invited a famous personality (deceased or living) to sit at your table for an interview. Who would you like to query? Brainstorm a list of factual, conceptual, and provocative questions to ask your guest. This example is tied to the generalization, "Mythical figures illuminate characteristics of good and evil."

Example: Santa Claus
Factual:
> Why do you think people perceive you as being a "jolly person?"
> Why do you give presents to children?
> What message do you have for children the world over?
> Why are you proud of your elves?
> Why is Rudolph your lead reindeer?

Conceptual:
> Why do many people believe in mythical figures?
> How do artists and writers shape perceptions of mythical characters?
> Why do mythical characters represent either good or evil?

Provocative:
> Is Santa Claus too materialistic? Should he switch from giving toys to solving problems such as global warming and scarce natural resources?
> Can one person's myth be another's reality?

Share questions by pairing tables if the group is large or share out loud by table if the group is smaller. The point of this learning experience is to see that participants can differentiate between the different kinds of questions, so humor is fine if they wish.

● *Differentiating Instruction With Conceptual Thinking*

Time: 40 minutes
Materials: Resource 17—Performance Modalities and Resource 9—Sample Conceptual Lenses

Choose a topic such as the American Revolution. Develop a learning experience for three modalities of performance selected from Resource 17. Select three conceptual lenses to focus the work in the different learning experiences. (In the classroom, students could choose the lens they would like to apply to their selected learning experience.)

● *Adapting Graphic Organizers*

Time: 25 minutes
Materials: Resource 18—Concept-Based Graphic Organizer

Review the graphic organizers on pages 192–193, which show an adaptation of a traditional graphic organizer to make it concept based. Review another example, Resource 18. Ask participants to name different graphic organizers they have used in their classroom, such as the "fishbone" or the "T-Chart." Ask participants to work with their group to "adapt" a traditional graphic organizer that they have used in their classroom to make it concept based. Have work groups share their favorite adaptation with the total audience.

● *Adapting Instructional Activities*

Time: 20 minutes
Materials: None

Ask participants to individually write out an activity they have used with their students that does not overtly use a concept (5 minutes). Then ask them to adapt the activity to bring in a conceptual level of work (5 minutes). Ask group members to share how they adapted their activities to make them concept-based learning experiences.

Journal Writing Prompts

You are applying for a teaching position in a school district that has a concept-based curriculum and instruction belief system. You are to answer the following question on your application:

"By observing your classroom and instruction, how will we be able to identify you as a concept-based teacher?"

Practical Applications

Take the suggestions from this chapter into your instruction. Practice the different strategies until they feel natural to your teaching. Think of new strategies to take students' thinking to the conceptual level and write them down. Share your ideas with fellow teachers and encourage them to develop concept-based ideas to share with you.

Extending Facilitator Learning

Buzan, T. (2002). *Mind maps for kids: Max your memory and concentration.* New York: Penguin.

Tomlinson, C. A., & Eidson, C. C. (2003a). *Differentiation in practice: A resource guide for differentiating curriculum, Grades K–5.* Alexandria, VA: Association for Supervision and Curriculum Development.

Tomlinson, C. A., & Eidson, C. C. (2003b). *Differentiation in practice: A resource guide for differentiating curriculum, Grades 5–9.* Alexandria, VA: Association for Supervision and Curriculum Development.

Tomlinson, C. A., & Strickland, C. A. (2005). *Differentiation in practice: A resource guide for differentiating curriculum, Grades 9–12.* Alexandria, VA: Association for Supervision and Curriculum Development.

Chapter 8. Stirring the Head, Heart, and Soul: Creating a Love of Learning

Summary

Quality teachers design learning environments and interact with students in ways that engage their minds and hearts. They realize that thinking students require thinking teachers. Thinking teachers do not feel a need to control student learning but create learning environments so that students can construct knowledge and develop personal understanding.

In this final chapter, Erickson describes how thinking teachers use brain-based strategies within a structure to help students become autonomous learners. She reinforces the need to teach process skills directly and to mastery. Finally, this chapter deals with the affective area of teaching and draws the reader into a profile of the passionate, caring teacher.

Discussion Questions

1. What kind of school or classroom environments discourage thinking teachers?
2. What kind of school or classroom environments encourage thinking teachers?
3. What kind of classroom environments discourage thinking students?

4. What kind of classroom environments encourage thinking students?
5. How do Gardner's multiple intelligences and Tomlinson's differentiation ideas stimulate the creative spirit of each child?
6. How would you describe the ideal learning environment for your students?
7. If you could identify a need for improvement in your classroom learning environment, what would it be? How can you create the change you need?
8. On a scale of 1 to 10, with 10 being a highly passionate learner, where would you place the majority of your students?
9. How significant is the teacher's affect and interaction with individual students in creating the love of learning?

Learning Experiences

● *Thinking Teachers*

Time: 30 minutes

Materials: Option—Resource 8— Unit Design Template (the last two pages)

Tell participants that thinking teachers develop thinking students, and in this learning experience they are invited to bring their thinking and creativity to design a lesson for students. Ask participants to think of a topic relevant to their curriculum and work together in a group of three to five people to design an engaging concept-based lesson. Put the following considerations on a chart or the board for the participants:

- Concept based (mandatory)
- Authentic—real world (optional)
- Differentiated to meet different learning needs
- Clear in directions to students
- The lesson must be concept based so you may want to remind the participants that this means there must be a conceptual lens or focus to the lesson. The lesson could be developed to meet a generalization drawn from the topic. Suggest that participants could use the lesson planner on pages 83–84 of the book (Resource 8—last two pages) if they wish.

● *Constructivist Learning*

Time: 10 minutes

Materials: Lesson plan developed in the Thinking Teachers Learning Experience

Lead participants in a discussion of constructivist learning. Ask why constructivist experiences are important in learning. Direct participants to review the table group lesson plan developed in the

Thinking Teachers Learning Experience and highlight which parts of the lesson engage students in *constructivist* learning. Then ask participants to evaluate whether the conceptual learning was drawn from students in the lesson summary and supported by the factual information. Share out loud any observations or reflections.

● *Stirring the Creative Spirit*

Time: 30–60 minutes
Materials: Easel paper, microphone, colored markers, any media or props the facilitator wishes to bring to the workshop

Tell participants that you value their creative spirit and want to close the workshop with a creative expression of what they have learned. Tell participants to work in their table groups to create a performance of some kind to share what they have learned with the total audience. Resource 17 can provide some ideas for different performance modalities, although there are many other options. Poetry, singing, drawings, cartoons, and speeches are just a few of the possible options. Tell the participants they have 30 minutes to develop the presentations and ____ minutes to present (depending on audience size).

This learning experience may not be feasible if the audience is too large because of time limits.

Journal Writing Prompts

You have been hired in the school of your dreams. Describe your ideal classroom in terms of the learning environment, the social/psychological environment, and your goals for your students.

Practical Applications

Evaluate your present classroom environment and determine how you could make it even closer to your ideal. Think of your relationship with each child. Choose one child that you would like to see making greater progress or a child that appears withdrawn. Make a special effort to connect with and verbally acknowledge your belief in and support for that child's efforts. Encourage that child and help him or her to succeed. Watch for changes in the child's efforts and affect within the next month.

As another option, concentrate on developing greater expertise with the brain-based, concept-based instructional strategies described in the book, and note on a monthly basis how students are showing greater evidence of higher-order thinking and engagement in their learning.

Extending Facilitator Learning

Brooks, J. G., & Brooks, M. G. (1993). *The case for constructivist classrooms.* Alexandria, VA: Association for Supervision and Curriculum Development.

Caine, R. N., & Caine, G. (1991). *Teaching and the human brain.* Alexandria, VA: Association for Supervision and Curriculum Development.

Caine, R. N., Caine, G., McClintic, C., & Klimek, K. (2005). *12 brain/mind learning principles in action: The fieldbook for making connections, teaching, and the human brain.* Thousand Oaks, CA: Corwin Press.

Eisner, E. (2004). *The arts and creation of mind.* New Haven, CT: Yale University Press.

Gardner, H. (2006). *Multiple intelligences: New horizons.* New York: Basic Books.

Resources

1. The Structure of Knowledge 37

2. Structure of Knowledge Example(s) 38

3. Blank Structure of Knowledge 39

4. Topic or Concept? 40

5. Supporting Universal Generalizations 41

6. Visual Interpretations 42

7. Unit Design Steps 43

8. Unit Planner and Lesson Planner 45

9. Sample Conceptual Lenses 51

10. Scaffolding Generalizations 52

11. Guiding Questions 53

12. Writing a Performance Task 54

13a. Elementary Grade Web 55

13b. Secondary Grade Level Web 56

14. Steps in Designing a Unit Web 57

15. Standard Level Performances for Critical Thinking 58

16a. Scoring Guide 59

16b. Scoring Guide for Primary Grade Task 60

16c. Scoring Guide for Task if Letter Grades Are Required 62

17. Performance Modalities 64

18. Concept-Based Graphic Organizer 65

Resource 1: The Structure of Knowledge

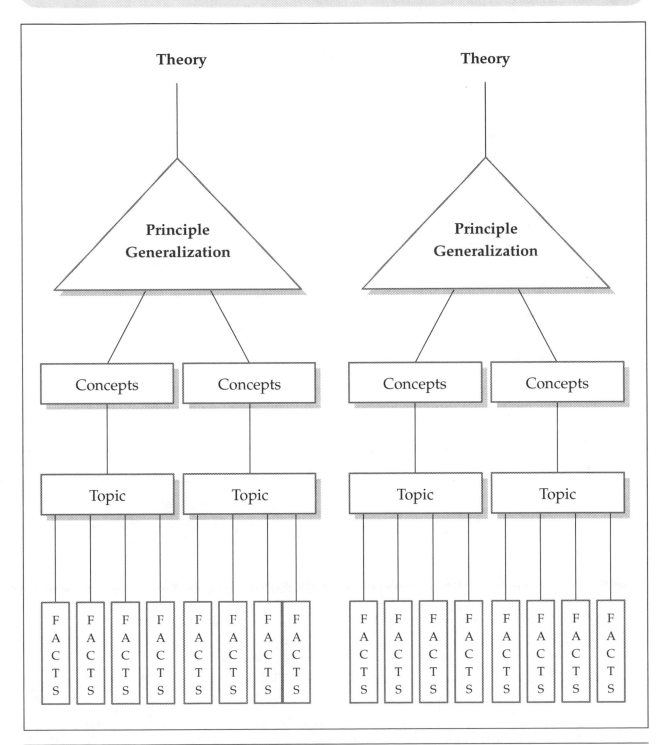

Resource 2: Structure of Knowledge Example(s)

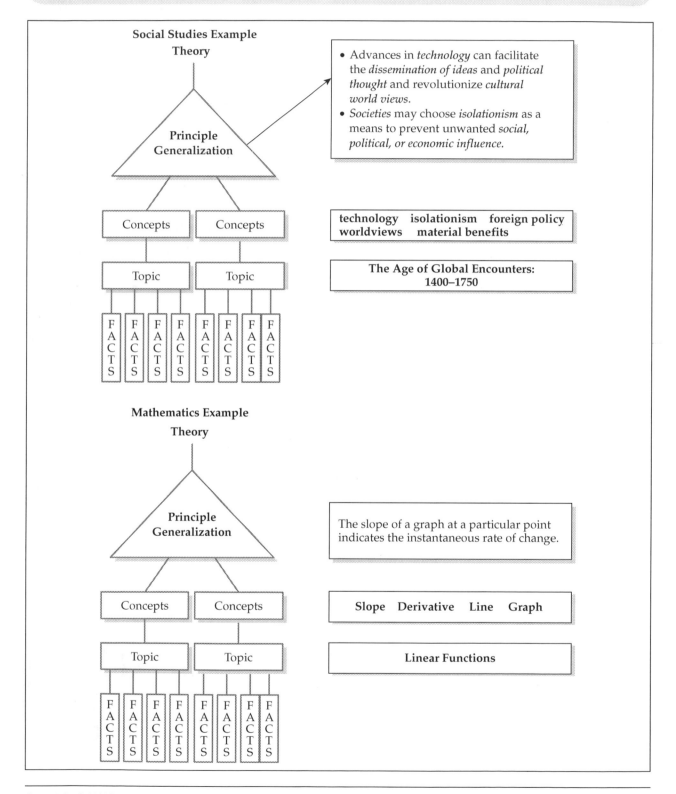

Social Studies Example
Theory

Principle Generalization

- Advances in *technology* can facilitate the *dissemination of ideas* and *political thought* and revolutionize *cultural world views*.
- *Societies* may choose *isolationism* as a means to prevent unwanted *social, political, or economic influence*.

Concepts   Concepts

technology   isolationism   foreign policy
worldviews   material benefits

Topic   Topic

**The Age of Global Encounters:
1400–1750**

FACTS FACTS FACTS FACTS FACTS FACTS FACTS FACTS

Mathematics Example
Theory

Principle Generalization

The slope of a graph at a particular point indicates the instantaneous rate of change.

Concepts   Concepts

Slope   Derivative   Line   Graph

Topic   Topic

Linear Functions

FACTS FACTS FACTS FACTS FACTS FACTS FACTS FACTS

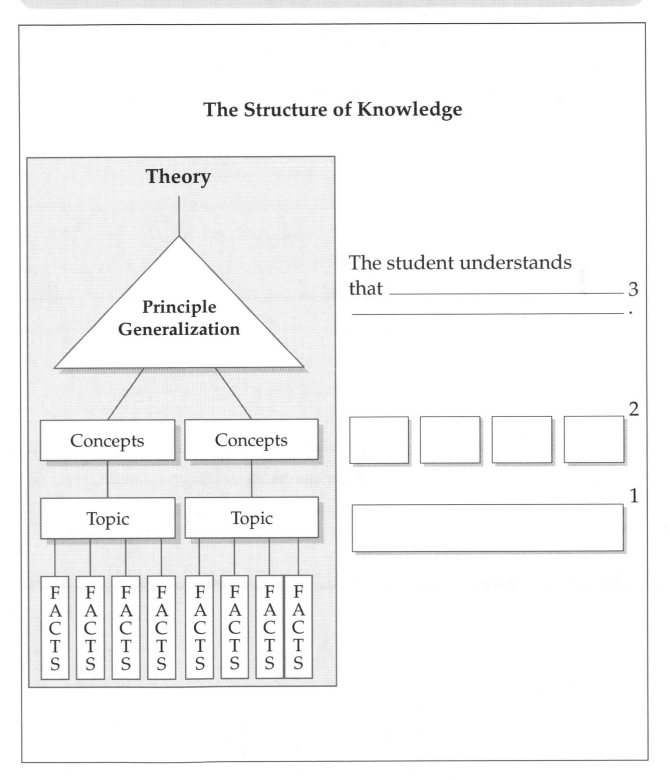

The Structure of Knowledge

Theory

Principle
Generalization

Concepts　Concepts

Topic　Topic

FACTS FACTS FACTS FACTS FACTS FACTS FACTS FACTS

The student understands that _____ 3.

2

1

Resource 4: Topic or Concept?

Topic or Concept?

✓ *the TOPICS*

George Washington

Alaska

Reptile

Multiplication

Organism

Cell

System

Relationships

Nairobi Desert

Internal Communications

Power

List 3 *topics* that you teach	List 3 *concepts* that you teach
1.	1.
2.	2.
3.	3.

In the list of checked topics above, circle 2 macroconcepts and
underline 2 microconcepts.

Supporting Universal Generalizations

*Write as many factual examples as you can think
of to support each of the following generalizations*

1. People migrate to escape oppression, to gain new opportunities, or for a sense of adventure.

2. Organisms adapt to changing external environments, or they will not survive.

3. Geometric shapes provide technical as well as aesthetic value in the natural and constructed world.

Resource 6: Visual Interpretations

Facts and Concepts

Reasons for changing the *emphasis* in instruction from <u>memorization</u> of facts, to the use of facts as a <u>tool</u> to develop deeper, conceptual understanding

Facts:

- The fact-based curriculum changes too rapidly

- A solely fact-based curriculum fosters lower-level thinking

- A fact-based curriculum maintains the fragmentation of knowledge

Concepts:

Universal concepts remain constant even though the fact base that supports the concepts may change over time.

Concepts foster the development of generalizations. Generalizations can be applied across the fields of knowledge.

Concepts and generalizations stimulate higher-level thinking by causing students to rise above the fact base to gain understanding.

Concepts and generalizations "integrate" thinking and allow for the transfer of knowledge.

Unit Components and Design Steps for a Concept-Based Unit of Study

1. Decide on a **unit title**.

   • The title is the centering topic for the study.

2. Identify a major **concept** to serve as a suitable **conceptual lens** for your study.

   • The conceptual lens draws thinking above the topic to the integration level. Integrated thinking sees the conceptual and transferable patterns and connections of knowledge.

   • Changing the conceptual lens changes the unit focus. For example, with the human body unit title, the lens could be "systems" or "structure."

3. Web the **subtopics** and **subconcepts** for study, by subject or area, around the concept and unit title.

   • **Subtopics** listed around this content planning web will be specific (e.g., "Amazon Rainforest" or "Early Americans"; **subconcepts** will be transferable (habitats, shelter, needs). Underline all subconcepts around the web. These will provide the fuel for writing generalizations.

4. **Write a unit overview** to engage student interest and introduce the unit. This step can be completed at the end of the unit writing process.

5. Brainstorm some of the **enduring, essential understandings** [*generalizations*] that you would expect students to derive from the study. (5–8 for elementary; 8–12 for secondary for a unit of study)

   • Generalizations answer the question, "So what? Why should I learn these facts?"

   • Generalizations go beyond the facts to the conceptual and transferable level of understanding. (This facilitates conceptual thinking and deep understanding.)

6. Brainstorm **"guiding questions"** to facilitate the student's study toward the enduring, essential understandings.

   • Guiding questions are factual and conceptual. A unit may also have a few *provocative*, debate questions, which have no right or wrong answer.

(Continued)

(Continued)

7. Identify the **specific knowledge** (*critical topics and/or facts*) **and skills** that students must internalize. "Students will 'know' factual knowledge and . . . 'be able to do' key skills . . . "

8. Code the knowledge and skills with **assessment codes** (AC) to show the other evidence that is planned beyond the performance tasks. Include these assessments in the unit packet.

9. Write a **culminating performance task** to show the depth of learning. Performance tasks answer the question, "What do I want students to know, understand and be able to do as a result of this unit of study?"

   • (You may develop 2 or 3 tasks for a 6-week unit if you wish)

   • Use the formula, "What," "Why," and "How" in writing to ensure that the performance measures learning to the conceptual level of deep understanding (the "Why" statement) .

10. Design the **scoring guide** (criteria and standard) to assess the performance task.

    • For each criteria assessed in a given mode, ask yourself, "What does it look like?" at the standard level of performance.

11. Design backward from the performance task(s) and write **learning experiences** to ensure student success on the performance task(s). Design other learning experiences to address the other unit requirements for *know, understand,* and *be able to do.*

12. Identify **unit resources** and include **teacher notes** to assist planning and instruction.

NOTE: The **Lesson Plan** pages on pages 83–84 in the book can be used to break down the unit plan into more manageable segments for instruction. The lesson plan may cover 3- to 5-day segments. A computer "copy and paste" method should work with some fleshing out of questions and learning experiences.

Critical Content/Concept Web

Unit Planner

Unit Title: _____

Conceptual Lens: _____

Unit Overview

Unit Title

Designer(s): _____   Grade Level: _____

Enduring Understandings (generalizations)	Stnd.	Guiding Questions
1.		1.
2.		2.
3.		3.
4.		4.
5.		5.

(Continued)

(Continued)

AC = Assessment Code

Q - Quizzes   P - Prompts
T - Tests   O - Observations
WS - Work Samples   D - Dialogues
SA - Student Self-Assessment

Critical Content and Skills

Students will know . . .	Stnd.	AC		Stnd.	AC
1.			4.		
2.			5.		
3.			6.		

Key skills . . .	Stnd.	AC		Stnd.	AC
1.			4.		
2.			5.		
3.			6.		

Step 1: *Task Planner*

What: Investigate . . .

Why: in order to understand that . . .

How: (Engaging Scenario-Performance)

Step 3: **Task Criteria**
(to be used for evaluation)

Scoring Guide for Primary Grade Task

Excellent **4** Meets and exceeds standard criteria:

Examples: Check box if met

S t a n d a r d | **Proficient** **3**

Developing 2 Meets 3/4 of the criteria in the standard
Novice **1** Nonscorable—Does not yet approach standard

(Continued)

(Continued)

Scoring Guide for task if letter grades are required

Possible points or percentages

Self assessment

Teacher assessment

Scoring Criteria

Content:

S t a n d a r d

Process:

Scoring Key

A =

B =

C =

I =

100 _____ _____

Suggested Learning Experiences

Correlations

Enduring Understanding

Know

Key Skill

1. _____

2. _____

3. _____

4. _____

5. _____

6. _____

7. _____

Unit Resources

Teacher Notes

(Continued)

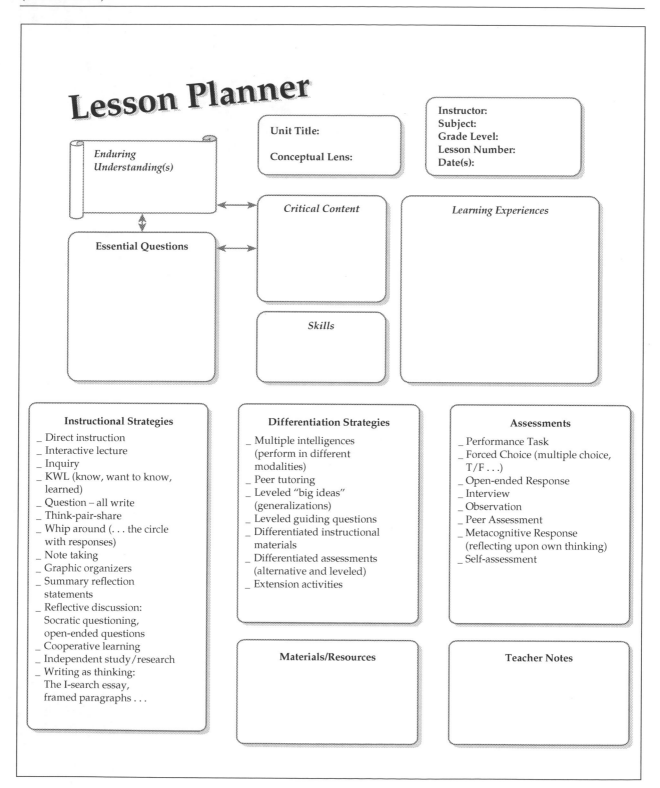

Lesson Planner

Enduring Understanding(s)

Unit Title:

Conceptual Lens:

Instructor:
Subject:
Grade Level:
Lesson Number:
Date(s):

Critical Content

Learning Experiences

Essential Questions

Skills

Instructional Strategies

_ Direct instruction
_ Interactive lecture
_ Inquiry
_ KWL (know, want to know, learned)
_ Question – all write
_ Think-pair-share
_ Whip around (. . . the circle with responses)
_ Note taking
_ Graphic organizers
_ Summary reflection statements
_ Reflective discussion: Socratic questioning, open-ended questions
_ Cooperative learning
_ Independent study/research
_ Writing as thinking: The I-search essay, framed paragraphs . . .

Differentiation Strategies

_ Multiple intelligences (perform in different modalities)
_ Peer tutoring
_ Leveled "big ideas" (generalizations)
_ Leveled guiding questions
_ Differentiated instructional materials
_ Differentiated assessments (alternative and leveled)
_ Extension activities

Assessments

_ Performance Task
_ Forced Choice (multiple choice, T/F . . .)
_ Open-ended Response
_ Interview
_ Observation
_ Peer Assessment
_ Metacognitive Response (reflecting upon own thinking)
_ Self-assessment

Materials/Resources

Teacher Notes

Resource 9: Sample Conceptual Lenses

Sample Conceptual Lenses

Conflict	Complexity
Beliefs/Values	Paradox
Interdependence	Interactions
Freedom	Transformations
Identity	Patterns
Relationships	Origins
Change	Revolution
Perspective	Reform
Power	Influence
System	Balance
Structure/Function	Innovation
Design	Genius
Aesthetic	Heroes
Force	Creativity

Scaffolding Thinking to Complex Levels

Level 3

_____

_____

So what is the effect or significance . . . ?

Level 2

_____

_____

<u>How</u> (or Why) . . . ?

Level 1

_____

_____

Guiding Questions

PROVOCATIVE (DEBATE): *Have no right or wrong answer.*
Cause students to debate and discuss.

Example: Should research on cloning be supported?

CONCEPTUAL: *Transfer through time, across cultures, and across situations.*
Use present tense verbs. Contain no proper nouns.

Example: Why do governments support scientific research?

FACTUAL: *Locked in time, place, or situation. May use present or past tense verbs.*
Often contain proper nouns.

Example: How did the research of Madame Marie Curie and Jonas Salk benefit mankind?

Resource 12: Writing a Performance Task

Performance Task Planner

What: Investigate (unit title or topic here) . . .

Why: in order to understand that . . . (generalization here):

How: (Engaging Scenario-Performance)

Unit Planner

Critical Content–Concept Web

"Interdependence"
(Conceptual Lens)

**Unit Title
"My Family"**

Culture
Education
Entertainment
and influence
on family
Holiday traditions
Families working
together
Values and beliefs

Economics
Budget and allowances
Jobs
Needs versus want
• shelter, clothing,
  food
• goods families
  consume
  (consumption)
Money
Goods and services

History
Families past and present
• ancestors; how did
  families work together?
Changing roles over time:
mother, father, children

Geography
Where families live
• migration
• influence of jobs
  on living location
• living locations of
  extended family
• effect of distance on
  family relationships:
  transportation;
  communication

Government
Types of governments
Regulations
• influence on family
  life/structure
Right/responsibilities
Family rules

Note: Concepts italicized

Unit Overview

Some families are large, some are small,
but your family is very important to you.
Your family takes care of you and helps
you meet your needs and wants.

Have you ever wondered . . . .
• Why families live in different cities?
• Why some of your relatives live in
  different locations?
• Why you have to follow rules?
• Why people use money?
• Why family members have to work
  together?
• What childhood was like for your
  parents and grandparents?
Let's find out!

Grade Level: First

SOURCE: Social Studies Committee, Meridian Joint School District No. 2, Meridian, Idaho; used with permission.

"System and Interaction"
(Conceptual Lens)

Atomic Structures
Valence electrons
Formation of ions
Electronegativity

Electronegativity
Periodic table trend
ionic/covalent continuum

Bond Types
Covalent, ionic, metallic
Polar covalent
Orbital hybridization
Sigma and pI bonds

Molecular Shape
VSEPR theory
Valence-bond theory
Polarity

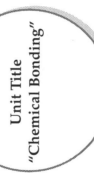

Unit Title
"Chemical Bonding"

Intermolecular Forces
London dispersion
Dipole-dipole
Hydrogen bonding

Bond Energy
Potential energy
Bond strength
Exothermic and end endothermic bonds

Modern Materials
Liquid crystals
Polymers
Ceramics

Compounds and Properties
Amorphous solid
Crystaline solid
- Molecular, ionic, atomic (liquids)
- Molecules with strong intermoleclar forces (gases)
- Molecules with weak intermolecular forces

Steps in Designing a Unit Web

1. Identify the *unit title* for the center circle on the web.

2. Identify a suitable *conceptual lens* to focus the unit work.

3. Identify the *strands* around the unit title.

4. List *subtopics* and *subconcepts* under each strand around the web.

Resource 15: Standard Level Performances for Critical Thinking

Standard Level Performances for Critical Thinking

CLARITY	LOGIC	ACCURACY
SIGNIFICANCE	PRECISION	BREADTH
DEPTH	FAIRNESS	RELEVANCE

Resource 16a: Scoring Guide

Scoring Guide

Culminating Performance

Performance
Level

4 - Expert
3 - Proficient
2 - Beginner
1 - Novice

4
3
_____ 2
1

4
3
_____ 2
1

4
3
_____ 2
1

4
3
_____ 2
1

Total Performance Score [ ]   Total Performance Level

_____ Expert
_____ Proficient
_____ Beginner
_____ Novice

Total Standard = 12
Criteria Standard = 3

Resource 16b: Scoring Guide for Primary Grade Task

Scoring Guide for Primary Grade Task

       Excellent   **4** Meets and exceeds standard criteria:

                      Examples: Check box if met

S t a n d a r d	**Proficient** **3**	☐
		☐
		☐
		☐

       Developing **2** Meets 3/4 of the criteria in the standard

       Novice   **1** Nonscorable—Does not yet approach standard

Task Engaging Scenario: Life Cycles

You are going to be "Teacher for a Day," and help younger students understand that . . .

        All living things go through life cycles.

How will you help students in Mrs. Jones' first grade class understand this idea?

1. Choose an organism to investigate.

2. Research the life cycle of your organism.

3. To display your findings you may choose one of the following:
   - Model of your organism's life cycle
   - Diagram
   - Poem
   - Creative story
   - Song
   - Cartoon strip
   - Dramatization

4. Using your products, partner with another student in your class who has chosen a different organism to research, and teach two students in Mrs. Jones' class that *all living things go through life cycles.* After you have each presented the life cycle of your organism, ask the younger students to tell how the life cycles are alike and different. Figure out a way to determine whether the younger students understand the idea that **all** living organisms go through a life cycle.

Scoring Guide for Primary Grade Task   **Scoring Guide for Product**

	Excellent	4	Meets and exceeds standard criteria:	
			Examples:	Check box if met

S t a n d a r d	Proficient	3	The life cycle stages are presented completely and accurately in the product. The product is well-designed or crafted:	☐
			- Clear depiction of life cycle	☐
			- Neat in appearance	☐
			- Thoughtfully crafted	☐
			- Creatively designed	☐

	Developing	2	Meets 3/4 of the criteria in the standard
	Novice	1	Nonscorable—does not yet approach standard

Scoring Guide for Presentation

Excellent	**4**	**Meets and exceeds standard criteria:** Examples: Highly creative and effective engagement of young learners - impact apparent on understanding and motivation	
			Check box if met

S t a n d a r d	Proficient	3	The presentation impact is evident:	
			- Younger students can identify likeness and differences between the two organisms.	☐
			- Younger students show understanding that all organisms go through life cycles.	☐
			The presentation to younger students is clear and focused:	
			- Explanations are clear	☐
			- Stays on topic	☐

	Developing	2	Meets 3/4 of the criteria in the standard
	Novice	1	Nonscorable—Does not yet approach standard

Resource 16c: Scouring Guide for Task if Letter Grades Are Required

Scoring Guide for Task if letter grades are required

Possible points or percentages

Self assessment

Teacher assessment

Scoring Criteria

Standard

Content:

Process:

☐	☐	☐
☐	☐	☐
☐	☐	☐
☐	☐	☐

Scoring Key
A =
B =
C =
I =

100 ____ ____

Step 1: Performance Assessment Planner: Hunter-Gatherers to Agrarians

What: *Investigate prehistory to 1000 BCE*

Why: *In order to understand that humans develop and continually improve on tools and technologies to provide for basic needs of food, clothing, and shelter.*

How: **(Engaging Scenario-Performance)**

As an archaeologist, you are fascinated by the development of early civilizations. You have agreed to make a presentation to the Trenton Historical Society on the topic "Early Civilizations: From Hunter-Gatherers to Agriculturalists."

1. *Research archaeological records for hunter-gatherer societies that existed prior to 1000 BCE in Africa and/or Western Eurasia.*

2. *Identify the factors that led humans from a hunter-gatherer lifestyle to an agrarian lifestyle.*

3. *Use a graphic organizer to compare how hunter-gatherer and agrarian societies met their basic needs for food, clothing, and shelter.*

4. *Develop a timeline showing the key factors and transition from hunter-gatherers to agrarian societies.*

5. *Prepare and present your talk, tracing the transition from hunter-gatherer to agrarian societies, to the Trenton Historical Society. Refer to evidence of artifacts and your visual aids to support your topic.*

Scoring Guide for Task if letter grades are required

Scoring Criteria	Possible points or percentages	Self assessment	Teacher assessment

S t a n d a r d

Content:

- Presentation clearly traces the transition from a hunter-gatherer to an agrarian society. | ☐ | ☐ | ☐
- The graphic organizer further clarifies and supports an understanding of the differences between hunter-gatherer and agrarian quests to meet basic needs. | ☐ | ☐ | ☐
- The timeline accurately depicts the key factors in the transition to an agrarian society. | ☐ | ☐ | ☐

Process:

- Oral presentation follows district guidelines: | ☐ | ☐ | ☐
  - Audible, clear voice
  - Interested emotional tone
  - Awareness of audience impact
  - Clear thesis statements with supporting evidence

Scoring Key
A =
B =
C =
I =

100 ____ ____

Resource 17: Performance Modalities

Task Products

Sculpture	Video clip	Round table discussion
Newsletter	Movie review	Experiment
Cartoon	Debate	Diorama
Advertisement	Action plan	Puppet show
Advertising jingle	Invention	Museum display
Fable; tall tale	Journal entry	Drawing
Letter	Critique	Story in song
Recipe	PowerPoint	Police bulletin
Quilt square	Model	Board game
Short story	Proposal	Map
Web page	Travel brochure	Biography

Resource 18: Concept-Based Graphic Organizer

Name _____

Date _____

Book Talk

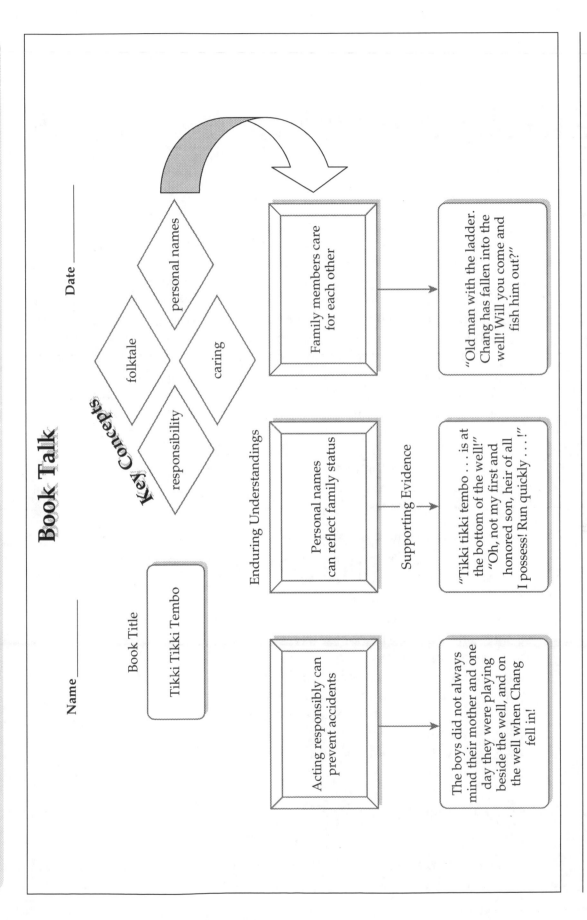

Key Concepts

- folktale
- personal names
- responsibility
- caring

Book Title

Tikki Tikki Tembo

Enduring Understandings

Family members care for each other

Personal names can reflect family status

Acting responsibly can prevent accidents

Supporting Evidence

"Old man with the ladder. Chang has fallen into the well! Will you come and fish him out?"

"Tikki tikki tembo . . . is at the bottom of the well!" "Oh, not my first and honored son, heir of all I possess! Run quickly . . . !"

The boys did not always mind their mother and one day they were playing beside the well, and on the well when Chang fell in!

Sample Workshop Agendas

In preparing for a workshop, facilitators will want to read the book, *Stirring the Head, Heart, and Soul: Redefining Curriculum, Instruction, and Concept-Based Learning,* and make notes to support the discussion questions and learning experiences they will be leading. They should answer the discussion questions for themselves to have an idea of possible audience responses.

The agendas that follow are suggestions and can be adapted if the facilitators desire to do so. Present the Workshop Overview as a set of guiding questions. You can assign times and show breaks for the workshop in a column beside the questions if you wish.

The following chapter learning experiences are not included in the suggested workshop agendas because of time constraints. They are included in the guide, however, as options in case a facilitator wishes to design a two-day workshop that does not complete the unit design process:

Chapter 1: Debating Ideas
Chapter 3: Examining the Design of State Academic Standards
Chapter 6: Let's Talk Testing
    A Thinking Rubric
Chapter 7: Fact-Based Versus Concept-Based Instruction
    The Power of Cooperative Learning
    Asking Powerful Questions
    Differentiated Instruction With Conceptual Thinking
    Adapting Graphic Organizers
    Adapting Instructional Activities
    Thinking Teachers
    Constructivist Learning

Agenda: Half-Day Workshop

Note to facilitator: In a half-day workshop your goals should be to lead a discussion on the need for a change in the design of curriculum, and teach the structure of knowledge and its significance in teaching and learning. You will engage participants in learning experiences that reinforce the power of a concept-based model, the structure of knowledge, the conceptual lens, and an introduction to unit design. Chapters 2, 4, and 5 and the related discussion questions further reinforce your presentation. Encourage participants to read further in the book after the workshop and practice the concept-based instructional strategies in their classrooms.

Welcome and Workshop Starter (10 minutes)
Workshop Overview Through Guiding Questions (5 minutes)
Chapter 2 (1 hour and 15 minutes)

Post the discussion questions for Chapter 2 to use with the learning experiences. (Facilitator: Read Chapter 2 for background information.) Guide participants through the Chapter 2 Learning Experiences:

1. The Structure of Knowledge using Resources 1, 2, and 3
2. Concept or Topic? using Resource 4
3. Universal Generalizations using Resource 5

Chapter 4 (30 minutes)

Engage participants with the Chapter 4 Learning Experience:

1. Choosing a Conceptual Lens using Resource 9

Chapter 5 (30 minutes)

Guide participants through the design of a unit web:

1. Designing a Unit Web using Resources 13a, 13b, and 14

Close the workshop with a summary of what was learned. Call for any remaining questions. Direct participants to page 75 in the book for a complete set of unit design steps if they wish to develop the entire unit. Encourage participants to practice the strategies learned with their students and teach other colleagues what they learned in the workshop. Ask participants to complete the workshop evaluation.

Agenda: One-Day Workshop

Welcome and Workshop Starter (10 minutes)
Workshop Overview Through Guiding Questions (5 minutes)
Note to Facilitator: In a one-day workshop, your goals should be the following:

- Emphasize the need for a change in the design of curriculum and instruction.
- Teach the structure of knowledge and its significance in teaching and learning.
- Engage participants in learning experiences that reinforce the power of a concept-based model: the structure of knowledge, the difference between topics and concepts, the difference between facts and generalizations, the conceptual lens, scaffolding generalizations, writing guiding/essential questions, and designing a concept-content unit web.
- Engage participants in specific instructional strategies that will develop the thinking abilities and increase motivation of their students.

Chapters 2, 4, and 5 and the related discussion questions further reinforce your presentation. Encourage participants to read further in the book after the workshop and practice the concept-based instructional strategies in their classrooms.

Chapter 2 (1 hour)

Post the discussion questions for Chapter 2 to use with the learning experiences. (Facilitator, read Chapter 2 in the book for background information.)
Engage participants with Chapter 2 Learning Experiences
1. The Structure of Knowledge—using Resources 1, 2, and 3
2. Concept or Topic?—using Resource 4
3. Universal Generalizations—using Resource 5

Chapter 4 (2 hours)

Engage participants with the Learning Experiences
1. Choosing a Conceptual Lens—using Resource 9
2. Writing Generalizations—using local state standards in a content area (avoid English/language arts "skills" for this learning experience)
3. Scaffolding Generalizations—using Resource 10
4. Writing Guiding/Essential Questions—using Resource 11

Chapter 5 (30 minutes)

Guide participants through the design of a unit web.
1. Designing a Unit Web—using Resources 13a, 13b, and 14

Close the workshop with a summary of what was learned. Call for any remaining questions. Direct participants to page 75 in the book for a complete set of unit design steps if they wish to develop the entire unit. Encourage participants to practice the strategies learned with their students and teach other colleagues what they learned in the workshop. Ask participants to complete the workshop evaluation.

Agenda: Two-Day Workshop

Welcome and Workshop Starter (10 minutes)
Workshop Overview through Guiding Questions (5 minutes)
   Note to Facilitator: In a two-day workshop your goals should be the following:

- Emphasize the need for a change in the design of curriculum and instruction.
- Teach the structure of knowledge and its significance in teaching and learning.
- Engage participants in learning experiences that reinforce the power of a concept-based model: the structure of knowledge, the difference between topics and concepts, the difference between facts and generalizations, the conceptual lens, scaffolding generalizations, writing guiding/essential questions, and designing a concept-based unit of instruction.
- Engage participants with specific instructional strategies that can be applied to developing the thinking abilities and increasing the motivation of students.

   Chapters 2, 4, 5, 6, and 7 and the related discussion questions further reinforce your presentation. Encourage participants to practice the concept-based instructional strategies in their classrooms.

After the welcome and workshop starter, review the workshop overview questions. Tell teachers that you will be asking them to form work groups of eight near the end of the day and will ask each member to choose a chapter to read, which they will report on within their work group in the morning. Tell them you will adjourn the workshop about 45 minutes early on this day to complete the reading.

Chapter 2 (1 hour)

Post the discussion questions for Chapter 2 in this facilitator's guide to use with the learning experiences. (Facilitator, read Chapter 2 in the book for background information.)

Engage participants with the Chapter 2 Learning Experiences:
   1. The Structure of Knowledge—Resources 1, 2, and 3
   2. Concept or topic?—Resource 4
   3. Universal Generalizations—Resource 5

Chapter 4 (2 hours)

Engage participants with the Chapter 4 Learning Experiences
1. Choosing a Conceptual Lens—Resource 9
2. Writing Generalizations—sample pages from state academic standards (facilitator provides)
3. Scaffolding Generalizations—Resource 10
4. Writing Guiding Questions—Resource 11

Chapter 5 (1 hour and 30 minutes)

Guide participants through the design of a unit web.
1. Designing a Unit Web—using Resources 13a, 13b, and 14

Ask participants to write at least two generalizations from their unit web before the day ends.
2. Writing Generalizations and Scaffolding Generalizations— combining concepts from the unit web as time allows in Day 1

If time permits, ask participants to write one set of factual and conceptual questions for one of the generalizations they just completed.
3. Guiding questions—using Resource 11 for one of the generalizations if time permits at the end of Day 1

Day 2—Next steps
After the book discussion, pick up on Day 2 by having participants refine and extend their work with generalizations and guiding questions. Then proceed onto the other unit components.

1. Book Discussion
2. Unit Design Continued:
   a. Unit web
   b. Generalizations
   c. Guiding questions
   d. Critical content (factual knowledge)
   e. Key skills
   f. Performance task
   g. Scoring guide
   h. Learning experiences
3. Stirring the Creative Spirit

Close the workshop with a summary of what was learned. Call for any remaining questions. Encourage participants to practice the strategies learned with their students and teach other colleagues what they learned in the workshop. Ask participants to complete the workshop evaluation

Workshop Evaluation Form

- How well did the workshop meet the goal and objectives?

- How will you apply what you learned during this workshop in your daily professional life?

- What professional support will you need to implement what you have learned from this workshop?

- How well did the topics explored in this workshop meet a specific need in your school or district?

- How relevant was this topic to your professional life?

- How well did the instructional techniques and activities facilitate your understanding of the topic?

- How can you incorporate the activities learned today into your daily professional life?

- Were a variety of learning experiences included in the workshop?

- Was any particular activity memorable? What made it stand out?

Context

- Were the facilities conducive to learning?

- Were the accommodations adequate for the activities involved?

Overall

- Overall, how successful would you consider this workshop? Please include a brief comment or explanation.

- What was the most valuable thing you gained from this workshop experience?

Additional Comments

SOURCE: Adapted from *Evaluating Professional Development* by Thomas R. Guskey, Corwin Press, 2000.

Notes

CORWIN PRESS

The Corwin Press logo—a raven striding across an open book—represents the union of courage and learning. Corwin Press is committed to improving education for all learners by publishing books and other professional development resources for those serving the field of PreK–12 education. By providing practical, hands-on materials, Corwin Press continues to carry out the promise of its motto: **"Helping Educators Do Their Work Better."**

Printed in the United States
By Bookmasters